The Flying Doctor

Alan Horsfield
Illustrated by Kevin Burgemeestre

Contents

The Royal Flying Doctor Service

Some people in Australia live in the outback, far away from towns and cities. It can take a long time for them to drive to a hospital if they are sick or injured. In 1928, a man named John Flynn started the Royal Flying Doctor Service. The Royal Flying Doctor Service uses airplanes to reach sick or injured people quickly and take them to the hospital. The Royal Flying Doctor Service operates 24 hours a day, 365 days a year.

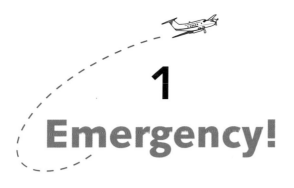

1
Emergency!

Randall Landers wiped his face. Even though he was wearing a hat, he knew he was probably still getting sunburned. The weather was so hot that he wished he could go for a nice, cool swim. There was a stream down below in the valley, but he had to keep up with the other riders. They were herding cattle.

It had been Randall's idea to help with the cattle today. His dad had finally agreed and let him take one of the horses out. But Randall was so hot now that he was almost sorry he had asked.

Looking up at the sky, he noticed dark clouds gathering behind the **mountain range** in the distance. Some light rain would be nice, but these clouds would bring very heavy rain.

They needed to get home quickly, but they were still a long way from home. As he took a gulp of water from his water bottle, his dad turned and gave him a friendly wave.

mountain range – a group of mountains

Then, just as Randall's horse was stepping around some rocks, something rustled in the grass. The horse jumped in fright. Randall tumbled off its back. He fell on his arm and shoulder and heard a cracking sound. He knew before he even felt the pain that a bone was broken.

Suddenly, Randall's dad was standing over him. Randall looked up at him. He could tell his dad was worried.

His dad yelled to Jim, one of the workers. "Quick! Ride home and get the truck. Tell my wife to call the Royal Flying Doctor Service. It's an emergency!"

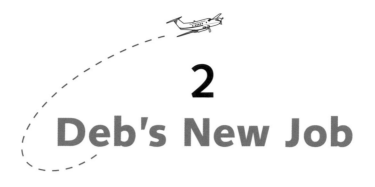

2
Deb's New Job

Meanwhile, many miles away, Deb's plane touched down on the runway. She was excited. She was starting a new job in a new place. First, she needed to introduce herself. Then she would find her new home, unpack, and settle in before beginning work the next day.

The plane rolled to a stop, and the exit door dropped down. Deb got out and walked over to the building. The climate in this part of Australia was very dry and hot. It felt very different from some of the places where she had worked before as a pilot.

A man was just putting the phone down when she walked into the building. "Hi. Are you Deb Nugent?" he asked.

"Yes, I am. I'm reporting for duty," she smiled.

"Hi! My name is Pete," he said, shaking her hand. "I know that you plan to start tomorrow, but one of our pilots is sick today. We just had a call from the Landers family. Their place is way out in the country. We need to get there quickly. It sounds like their son has broken his arm. Can you be ready to fly the plane in thirty minutes? Doctor Mulroy will be going along with you."

"Sure. It looks like I got here just in time!" said Deb.

"You sure did!" said Pete. "Doctor Mulroy knows this part of the country and will help you find your way there. She's gone out to the plane already. It has a full tank of gas and is ready to go. Here's the map and the directions."

"Thanks! I'll go right away," smiled Deb, opening the door.

Doctor Mulroy was waiting by the plane.

"Hi! I'm Doctor Mulroy," she said, holding out her hand to shake Deb's. "I see they've got you working already!"

"Yes. Nice to meet you, Doctor. I'm Deb," she said. "I'm glad you know the area. I'll need some help finding the way!"

Deb checked the plane. Everything looked fine. Then she spent a few minutes looking at the map with Doctor Mulroy.

"I think we can take off now," smiled Deb to Doctor Mulroy. "Climb on board."

Deb climbed into the pilot's seat, and Doctor Mulroy sat next to her.

As Deb taxied down the runway, she noticed storm clouds gathering in the sky over the mountain range in the east, right where she was heading. She hoped that the weather wouldn't be a problem.

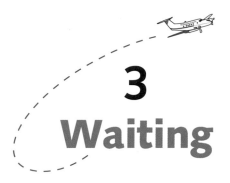

3
Waiting

Randall's dad gazed across the plains,
looking for Jim and the truck. Then he
looked over at Randall, who was sitting
in the shade of a tree.

"Jim should be back any minute, son,"
he said. "Hang in there."

He gave a sigh of relief when he saw
the growing dust cloud coming toward
them. The truck was here at last! They'd
waited less than thirty minutes in the shade
of a tree. There wasn't much water left,
and he was anxious to put some ice on
Randall's arm to bring the swelling down.

"A doctor from the Royal Flying Doctor Service is on the way!" shouted Jim as he parked the truck.

Randall's father helped him into the truck, trying to keep his arm as still as possible.

Jim drove carefully back to the house across the red, dusty ground. He tried to avoid rocks and holes. Every bump made Randall wince.

Randall's mother was waiting outside the house when they got home. She had a big glass of water and an ice pack ready.

"My poor boy! How are you feeling?" she asked when the truck pulled up. "Here, have some water."

Randall's father scanned the sky for the plane. There were dark thunderclouds in the sky and the sun was sinking fast. He knew that landing in poor light could be dangerous.

"There's the plane!" cried Randall's mother, pointing to a silver glint above the horizon.

Randall's father sighed with relief.

4
Rescue!

Doctor Mulroy had helped Deb find the way by pointing out **landmarks** on the ground below.

"It's such bare country," said Deb. "There are hardly any trees or bushes at all. It's very different from where I lived before."

They were almost there. Deb could see the airstrip ahead of her. Storm clouds towered above, hiding the sun that was almost setting. There was no time to waste. The storm was coming.

But just as Deb got ready to land the plane, she saw some animals on the airstrip. Some kangaroos had come out at dusk and

---

landmarks – things on the land that are easy to find and identify

were hopping all over the place! She flew low over the airstrip, hoping the noise would scare them away. She was glad to see them hop off into the distance.

She turned back again and brought the plane in for a smooth, but dusty, landing.

"Perfect!" said Doctor Mulroy.

"Thanks for your help, Doctor," said Deb.

Within moments, Doctor Mulroy was out of the plane checking Randall's injuries. She cleaned Randall's cuts and tested for pain. She made a temporary sling to hold his arm, tying it tight so that it couldn't move around.

"You'll need some help getting on board," she said to Randall. "You won't need to lie down, so you'll be able to look out the window."

"Thanks," said Randall. He was feeling a little better already.

Randall's dad and Jim lifted Randall into a seat. Dad carefully fastened Randall's seat belt before he got off the plane. Then Randall's mom climbed up and strapped herself into a seat.

Deb got into the pilot's seat and prepared for take-off.

"Have a safe trip," called Randall's dad.
Deb shut the door and the propellers whirled.
Just as the plane took off, the rain started.

5
Racing the Storm

Randall could hardly see his dad waving goodbye below. The rain was beating down as the plane climbed into the sky. Thunder boomed and lightning flashed over the mountain range. Soon his house disappeared from view. But he could see the dusty dirt road that linked their land to the highway.

"How are you feeling?" Deb called over the noise of the plane.

"Okay," Randall called back. "But it still hurts."

"We'll get you to the hospital as soon as we can," she shouted.

"Thanks!" shouted back Randall's mom.

A few minutes later, Doctor Mulroy went up to talk to Deb at the front of the plane.

"I'm trying to outrun the storm," Deb said to her quietly. "I don't like the look of that lightning."

A strong gust of wind made the plane drop suddenly. Everyone gasped.

"It's okay," said Deb. "There might just be a few bumps!"

There was very little light left. Rain beat on the windows.

To the north, Deb could just see the peaks of the mountains. She checked her map. They weren't far from the airport now. They were going to arrive before the worst part of the storm caught up with them. Deb was relieved.

Soon Deb saw the dim lights of the town through the rain. Next, she saw the runway lights of the airport. It was a welcome sight.

"We're almost there!" she called.

6
Safe at Last

Deb landed the plane and taxied to the airport. An ambulance was waiting.
In a few minutes, Randall was moved to the ambulance. Doctor Mulroy and his mom got in with him.

"You'll feel better in no time," Deb smiled at Randall as he sat in the ambulance.

"Thank you," said Randall. "It must be exciting to fly a plane."

"Sometimes it can be a little too exciting!" said Deb. "It was an interesting day in a new place."

"Come and visit us when we return home," Randall's mom said.

"Yes, when I'm better we can go riding together," Randall suggested.

"That's a great idea!" said Deb. "See you soon!"

Deb watched the ambulance drive away. She looked up at the sky, and at the strange, different land around her. "I think I'm going to like it here," she thought, smiling to herself.

The Australian Outback

Australia is a big country. Most of the middle of Australia is called the outback. It is dry, hot land that is far from cities and towns. The outback has some of Australia's largest cattle ranches. They are called *stations*. Some of the stations are larger than the state of Delaware!

These cattle live on a station in the outback.

Think About the Story

In *The Flying Doctor*, Randall breaks his arm and is rushed to a far-away hospital by airplane. Think about these questions.

- What features of the land does Randall think about just before he breaks his arm?
- Why do Randall's parents call the Royal Flying Doctor Service?
- Why is Deb worried about flying through the storm?

To learn more about interesting places in the world, read the books below.

SUGGESTED READING
Windows on Literacy
Down the Nile
Grand Canyon Adventure

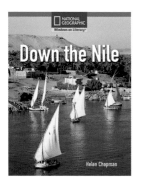

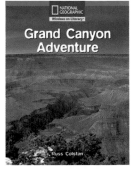